Visit our website at www.skyhorsepublishing.com.

10 9 8 7 6 5 4 3 2

Library of Congress Cataloging-in-Publication Data is available on file.

Cover design by Daniel Brount
Cover photo credits: Chelsey Brown, Natalia Rowe, and Nicole Blackmon

Print ISBN: 978-1-5107-5813-1
Ebook ISBN: 978-1-5107-5814-8

Printed in China

RENTAL STYLE

THE ULTIMATE GUIDE TO DECORATING YOUR APARTMENT OR SMALL HOME

CHELSEY BROWN

FOREWORD BY KIMBERLY DURAN

Skyhorse Publishing

FOR RHONDA, BRUCE, GRANDMAY, AND PAPA

CONTENTS

FOREWORD

From my early twenties through to my early thirties, I lived in about fifteen different rental properties. From a tiny bed shoehorned into what could only be described as a closet in a shared house in Denver to a fifty-square-foot flat four stories up at the top of a Victorian house in Allentown, Pennsylvania, to an open-plan but incredibly bland apartment in a tiny town in Wisconsin, I've experienced my fair share of shifty landlords, swirly patterned carpet, and bathrooms so small you had to sit sideways.

No matter what the situation, however, I always felt strongly about making whatever roof I had over my head a home. I remember having a print of *Flaming June* by Frederic Lord Leighton in an ornate gold frame that I carted around with me to each and every one of those rental homes through the entirety of the nineties, believing, if nothing else, it would make the space feel more like my own.

Every apartment became a learning curve with new challenges to overcome. Little by little, I learned a few tricks to make a space more comfortable, to create a sanctuary that I was happy to come home to. Soon, friends asked me to help them decorate their own rentals, and I even had the odd landlord ask me for advice to make their rentals more appealing to the market after seeing what I had done to transform the ones I'd lived in.

Two decades on, and I've left the United States for England, where I own my home—but the lessons I learned while apartment-dwelling have never left me. Houses here are, on average, much smaller than in the United States, and so I've had to get creative all over again with whatever space I have available to me.

I am not a trained interior designer, and I'm guessing if you are reading this book, then you may not be either. The truth is, armed with a bit of knowledge, I believe anyone can be their own designer and transform just about any property into a comfortable, personality-filled space (without losing your deposit!).

I've been blessed to have my home featured in four interior design books, twenty different magazines across the world. I've also been asked to give talks and interviews on interiors to thousands of people at events, on national radio, and podcasts. My blog, *Swoon Worthy*, which shares my own journey to creating a home with millions of people worldwide, has graciously won multiple industry awards.

I say these things not to boast but to show you, dear reader, that even someone without formal schooling can find success in creating a beautiful home. In short, if I can do it, anyone can.

While we've yet to meet "in real life," I've known Chelsey for quite a few years (the beauty of social media!) and have watched her grow in confidence as a designer. I've watched her blog become an important and authoritative voice in a world where there are few acknowledging the challenges of interior design in a rental space. I've seen her launch product lines and use every trick of the trade to resounding success in the apartments she's transformed.

During my time living in countless different flats, I wish I had a resource like *Rental Style* in hand.

Today, a wealth of products is available to renters that allows you to temporarily transform what you might think you are stuck with. Chelsey willingly shares that product knowledge with you, creating what reads like a little black book of her top resources and secrets, from budget buys to luxury looks for less than you might think.

Chelsey's book is a bit like having a friend hold your hand as she walks you through the sometimes turbulent and stressful world of apartment living. Step by step and room by room, her guidance and reassurance can truly transform any rental property into a thing of beauty. She takes the fear and uncertainty of what you can and can't do out of the equation, arming you with the knowledge required to make success of any space.

We know from so many studies that where you live has an incredible impact on your well-being. Making the investment in either time or money to make your rental property into your personal sanctuary allows you to feel content and happy as soon as you walk through the door. Even better, it becomes a place that reflects and celebrates you and your story.

I no longer own that *Flaming June* print, sadly, having left it behind when I moved across the Atlantic so many years ago. Looking back, I wish I had brought it with me, because it represented my own story and my wish to make my own mark. It also represented the most important lesson of all: that no matter where you live, adding your own personality to a rental space is always a good idea.

—Kimberly Duran
www.swoonworthy.co.uk

PREFACE

For the past few years, I have been dedicated to helping others create their dream home out of a rented space. Why, you ask? When researching interior design tips or reading interior design books, I was concerned that most of the information focused on larger spaces or designing a space you owned. Furthermore, many of the helpful tips and products in those resources were not very accessible (budget-wise) to the average person. This didn't seem right when you consider there are more renters now than at any time within the past five decades.

It pains me to hear people say, "Why bother when I'm just moving out in a year or two?" You should bother because even though you don't own the space, it's still your home. It's the place you come back to after a hard day's work. It's where you entertain your friends, relax, and feel most comfortable. The space around you can easily define your mood. A messy, uninteresting home will put you in a funk every time you walk in and out the door.

Likewise, many people are afraid to put effort into their rented space because they are fearful of renter restrictions that can leave their home bland and boring. My goal is to erase that unease and show you that you can turn a rented space into a home using temporary, creative tricks that won't drive your landlord crazy.

The budget and time-friendly tools, tips, and advice in this book will give you the ability to meet your goals and stand out among the rest. So, what are you waiting for? It's time to **revamp your rented space**.

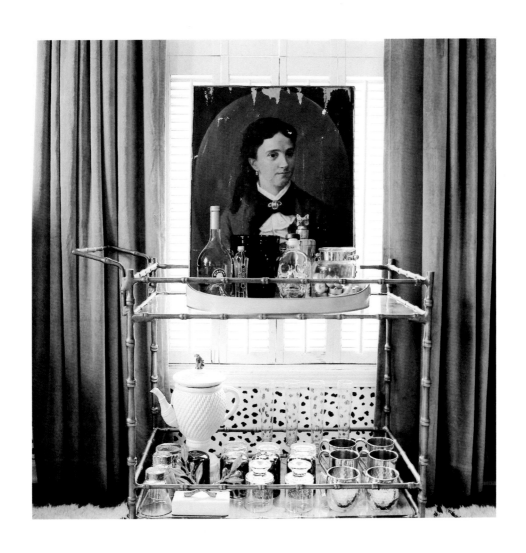

Has your landlord forbidden you from painting, but you have a color you can't get out of your mind? Have no fear! You can buy white, removable wallpaper that's meant to be painted over. It will remove easily upon moving out—and keep your landlord happy.

FINDING A HOME

By far, one of the most stressful times in my life was searching for my first apartment in Manhattan. I spent many days visiting apartment after apartment, only to realize that none of them met any of my necessary requirements. In those scarce one or two instances where I did find a home I liked, it was immediately taken off the market before I could even put down a deposit. As a last resort, I employed a broker to show me more options. The first apartment he took me to ended up being a winner, and I signed the lease immediately.

That anxiety-ridden time ended up being a significant learning moment for me. From that experience, I learned the dos and don'ts of searching for an apartment in a large metropolitan city.

1. If possible, find a no-fee home.

Usually, brokers will make you sign a contract that obligates you to pay them 7 percent or more of your entire yearly rent when you sign a lease. If you want to use a broker, make sure they first show you no-fee* apartments where the landlord pays their fee. Nowadays, there are many resources and websites that easily allow you to search for no-fee apartments. Start browsing these websites at least three weeks before you want to move. This takes me to my next tip.

2. Do not wait until the last minute.

Your choices might be limited if you're searching for an apartment at the last minute. Landlords and management companies usually know their inventory thirty days before a vacancy. Signing for your next home weeks in advance will not only guarantee you have a home but also ensure less stress and anxiety.

3. Sign as soon as possible.

In large cities like New York City and Chicago, apartments go *quickly*. You can view a listing in the morning, and it can be gone by the late afternoon. The market moves so incredibly fast that you have to make decisions on the fly. If you like a home, the biggest mistake you can make is to mull over the apartment for a few hours or a few days. Chances are, by the time you've decided that you want it, it will already be gone. I know; it has happened to me!

---

* A "no-fee" apartment means that the renter does not have to pay a broker's fee.

Acrylic or lucite
furniture can make
a smaller space feel
less cluttered and
more open.

4. Keep the right paperwork on hand.

Whether you have a guarantor (someone who meets the income requirement if you don't) or not, make sure to have all the necessary paperwork ready. Usually, landlords or management companies will request a photo ID, pay stubs, and at least one or two checks for a deposit and first month's rent. Not having these items on hand could allow someone else to snatch up the apartment before you do.

5. Remember to measure.

Whether you're recycling old furniture or buying new, it's essential to make sure you know the measurements of the home you're about to lease. If you don't have a tape measure on hand, make sure to get an exact floor plan with measurements. This will ensure your existing or planned furniture will properly fit.

6. Don't limit your neighborhood.

Keep an open mind! Only looking at one neighborhood significantly limits your choices. An apartment a few blocks from where you're looking can be hundreds of dollars less.

BEFORE

MOVING IN /

You've signed for your new home and are absolutely ecstatic about it. Before you move from your "old" place and start packing, there are a few things you should do beforehand. You need to decide what items you're taking with you and what items you're buying. What do you want the interior style of your next home to be? If you're buying most of your furniture, you want to make sure it will all fit before pressing that order button. We'll get to that a little later.

If starting fresh, the best place to begin is with your bases. Your bases are large pieces of furniture like a sofa, bed, area rug, and any other large items of furniture. Smaller items, like decor and art, can be figured out once you've moved in.

Protruding windowsills are great surface spaces to utilize for decor and storage.

Little storage boxes make a big difference in a smaller space. These decorative items are perfect for storing smaller items, such as jewelry.

A narrow console table is the perfect addition to any smaller space. It can be utilized as a desk, dining table, or a place to display decor.

When renting, you can invest in some items that will last for years, but there are some items you should consider re-buying after a year or two. I'll discuss bedroom furniture later, but let's first start with the basics.

Mirrors.

Invest. This entails wall and floor mirrors. A mirror is an item that's rarely touched and therefore less likely to show wear. It's also an item that you can reuse and take with you when you have to eventually move.

Couch.

Do not invest. If the living room is the primary area of gathering in your home, your sofa will be heavily used and challenging to clean over time no matter how hard you try to take care of it. I'm not saying to go out and buy a $100–$200 couch (unless you find it super comfortable!), but definitely don't spend thousands on one.

Wall Art.

Invest. Like a mirror, wall art is something rarely touched and therefore less likely to become damaged or dirty over time. Art is something you can take with you from home to home and even pass down to future generations.

Coffee Table.

Do not invest. This is an item that is virtually used all the time. It always has drinks, food, books, shoes—you name it—on it! Not only is it going to get dirty very quickly, but it's also going to get scratched over time; that's something not easily fixable. Don't necessarily spend fifty dollars on one, but don't go out of your way spending hundreds.

Area Rugs.

Do not invest. Your rugs are going to get soiled over time no matter how often or hard you try to clean them. It's not realistic to have guests remove their shoes every time they come into your home. Therefore, it may not be prudent to spend hundreds of dollars on a nice rug when it's just going to get ruined over a short time period. Also, it's near to impossible to remove germs from rugs! The best approach is to find and buy a new, budget-friendly rug once every year or two.

Decor.

Do not invest. Even though decor is rarely touched, it's something you might want to constantly switch out due to seasons or even developing a new interior style. You may love a piece of decor now, but you also may get tired of it after a few months.

Curtains.

Invest. Curtains are so important for not only the look of your space, but also the functionality of it. Are you in need of curtains to block out light or let light in? With curtains, most of the time, you get what you pay for in terms of fabric. Investing in good panels will ensure your space looks beautiful while still being functional.

Don't be afraid to place objects behind one another on a shelf. This adds dimension and character!

HOLY BIBLE New INTERNATIONAL VERSION INTERNATIONAL BIBLE SOCIETY

THE DA VINCI CODE   DAN BROWN   Doubleday

Once you've decided what bases you want, reach out to your landlord or management company and request one more viewing before you move in. That day, bring your furniture measurements, a tape measure, and painter's tape. Plot out exactly where you want your furniture to go with the tape. This will visually show you how the spacing will feel once items are moved into the apartment.

Moving day is a combination of the strangest emotions. You're excited to move into a new space, but you're also insanely stressed having to get all your furniture up four flights of stairs. Moving in a large city with street parking restrictions is not an easy task! I remember the stress of my dad having to drive around the block twenty-five times because there was no place to park on the street. If you can afford it, consider using a moving company.

Now that all of your items are moved in, what do you do next? It's time to make this rented space your *home*.

Hardware.

Landlords will usually install unflattering hardware because of cost. Switching out cabinet knobs and handles can immediately give your space a chic, modern upgrade.

Blinds and curtains.

Raise your hand if you've ever rented an apartment with stunning blinds already installed. I can't see you, but I know no one is holding up their hand! Covering the blinds with curtains can instantly make your space feel more homey.

Shower head.

Most apartments will have simple, low-pressure shower heads to conserve water. Depending on your personal beliefs on environmental issues, you may want to switch out your shower head to one that is massaging, higher pressure, or even lower pressure, to best fit your needs.

Light fixtures.

Switching out your ceiling light fixtures can create a dramatic transformation to your space with minimal effort. Affordable light fixtures can be found at the big-box stores like Home Depot or online at Wayfair or Amazon.

Just make sure to keep all the original landlord-provided hardware in boxes so you can switch them back once you move out.

HOME BODY

JOANNA GAINES

MANOLO BLAHNÍK

the COVETEUR

SHE

kate spade ♦ new york

THE

As a renter, you've probably heard many myths throughout the years about landlords, management companies, lease agreements, and more. Today, I am going to break most of those myths. In fact, after you read this, renting might be a little less scary.

It's legally binding if it's in the lease.

You would think this is true because a lease is a legal contract; however, this can be false. If a lease goes against city or state laws, it cannot be binding. If you're moving to a new city or state, make sure you look into its specific renter laws.

You won't get an apartment with a bad credit score.

Yes, it's true that having a bad credit score can make finding an apartment more difficult. However, filling out an application with a roommate, guarantor, or letters of recommendation can significantly help improve your chances of being accepted for a property.

You can't nail into walls.

This is completely false. In most rented spaces, you can use nails as long as you patch up the holes when you move out. However, you should still try to use nail-free removable hooks wherever possible! Make sure to review with your landlord ahead of time to discuss their preferences.

Your landlord can evict you for any reason.

Most states have tenant protection laws stating that a landlord needs sufficient evidence to break the lease agreement unilaterally. Don't worry—you won't suddenly find all your belongings out on the street without due process!

You can't change rental prices.

Usually rental prices are set in stone; however, there are a few ways to bargain and possibly decrease your monthly payment. One of those ways is to negotiate a longer lease with your landlord. Usually, you can get a rental decrease if the landlord or management company knows you will be staying for more than two years.

Landlords can enter whenever they want.

Legally, a landlord can't enter your apartment without giving twenty-four hours' notice (in most states). Exceptions to this are emergencies such as a fire or flood within the home. In addition, landlords do have the right to enter the property when they wish to show it for sale or rent. However, there should be a clause in the lease that states the process for showings. If it's not in the lease, you can request a clause to be put in before you sign.

Usually, landlords and management companies just want to keep you happy so you'll stay for a few years. Likewise, it's important to keep on your landlord's good side as they are your go-to resource for any issues that may arise in the home.

Your first instinct in a small apartment is usually to place furniture against a wall. However, floating your furniture will allow you to designate separate areas and maximize the space.

ENTRYWAY OR HALLWAY

Want to add an extra-unique feel to your rental home? Cover your doors with removable wallpaper!

Your entryway is the first part of your home people will see when they walk through your door. First impressions are always important, which means you'll want to create a statement that people will remember.

The trick with any entryway is to make it stylish yet functional. The number-one rule is to always hang a mirror here. A mirror will add some glam character and make your space feel bigger. It's also a way to check yourself before heading out the door or a secondary space for your guests to primp (if you live in a smaller home).

Another important element is including some sort of cabinet or console table. The surface of this piece can be styled with decor, books, and art that reflect you. For example, you can stack a couple of books and place some accents on top or place a large decorative bowl in between candles. The possibilities are endless. Try not to overdo it so you'll have enough space left over for miscellaneous items like keys or notes.

Every entryway needs an interior statement. This can either be a fun chair next to your console table or some wall decor on either side of your mirror. You can even place a fun or unusual rug (like cowhide) under your console and make that your feature element.

If your landord approves, you can also switch out the light fixture that's already in your entryway. If you don't have one, then think about incorporating a plug-in swag light!

Narrow hallways are similar to entryways in that there should always be an interior statement in this space. Many people neglect to decorate their small hallways, which, in turn, makes them feel even tinier. When it comes to decorating a hallway, focus on the floors and walls. A simple narrow runner and wallpaper can turn a bland hallway into one of your favorite spaces in your home.

REMOVABLE PRODUCTS MEANT FOR RENTERS

Being a renter means having to deal with a few restrictions that may leave decorating a bit of a struggle. Whether it's hanging up artwork damage-free or wanting to replace ugly flooring, these projects seem almost impossible to complete. Well, now that we live in a world where the renter market is growing, so are the renter-friendly products that are available! Below are some fantastic removable products that you will want to utilize in your own rented space:

- Removable wallpaper (think of it like a big sticker!)
- Removable backsplash (you can find almost any pattern on the market)
- Removable hooks (place some in your entryway to hang keys, bags, etc.)
- Removable floor tile (yes, this does exist!)
- Removable Velcro tape (these products are a perfect substitute for nails)

Unfortunately, many apartments don't include a proper foyer or entryway. Some of those homes only include an entryway that is simply just a narrow hallway. Here are a few tips on how you can create a stunning entryway in a very narrow space.

Incorporating a runner.

Adding a runner to your narrow entryway will help draw the eye forward. Just make sure the rug is durable and has a non-slide pad underneath, as this is a high-traffic area.

Adding interest to the walls.

As this is the first area people will see when they walk into your home, it's important to include wall accents that complement the rest of your space. When choosing wall art and decor, it's important to utilize the vertical space you do have and hang items high. This draws the eye upward and creates the feeling of a larger space. I also suggest using white and neutral colors, as they'll make the space feel brighter and more open.

The floors and walls are key decorating points to focus on in a narrow hallway or entryway.

Hanging a floating shelf.

Have no room for a console table? You can still add surface space by installing a small, narrow shelf. This is a great area to place small items like keys and sunglasses.

Incorporating hooks.

If you live in a smaller space, hooks are essential in your entryway. This will give you and your guests a dedicated spot to place coats and bags versus having these items scattered across the home.

Adding a mirror.

In addition to adding wall accents, you should try and include a mirror in this space. A mirror will always make your space feel larger than it actually is.

LIVING ROOM

If you're living in a smaller space, such as an apartment, I'm guessing you probably have a tiny living room. This room is pretty much the only space where you and your guests can gather, which makes it an important area. The living room should not only reflect your personal style and be a decorative statement about your home, but should also serve as a comfortable and functional space for you and your guests.

The key to turning a small area into a luxe living space is to trick the eye into making the space larger than it actually is. This can be achieved by using neutral colors, natural light, and large mirrors. Additionally, furniture made from lucite or acrylic can create the same illusion.

Always make sure to decorate your coffee table if you live in a smaller home. This is a perfect area to show off your unique style!

A coffee table is the heart and center of any living room, especially if you're living in a smaller space. It needs to be not only stylish, but also functional for constant use.

Books.

This has to be the golden tip for any coffee table. Books are fabulous as decor and conversation starters. Make sure your coffee-table books relate to you or your hobbies in some way. I personally like to stick to books that revolve around interior design or fashion. You can also choose books based on certain color tones.

Something tall.

Coffee tables are low pieces of furniture that can be enhanced by adding an element of height. A tall candle or piece of decor would definitely do the trick.

Something small.

Make sure to have one or two pieces of small decor to place on top of your books. When choosing the right accents, you want to make sure they complement the overall style of the room.

Flowers.

Consider a nice vase of flowers or a plant. They don't necessarily have to be real— faux flowers will work perfectly fine!

In addition to the tips above, it's important not to overdo it with the decor. You don't want your table feeling cluttered, especially if you're living in a small space. The key is to make sure that there is still enough room on the surface for drinks and some food—remember, it is a table after all!

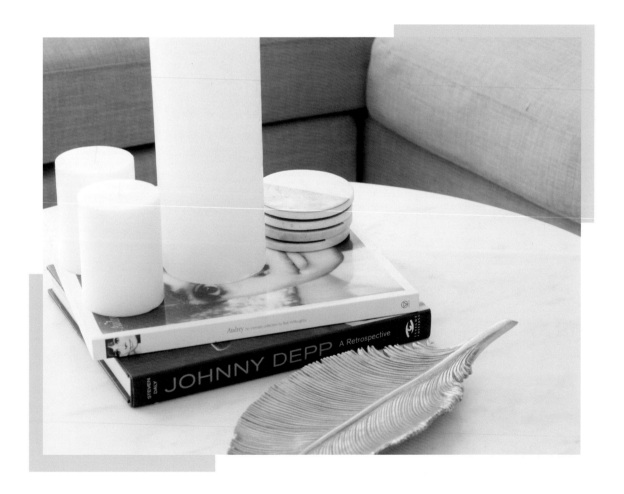

Radiator covers work perfectly for decorative function and additional surface space.

Need to cover up an ugly radiator? You can paint it, or add a shelf above to disguise it.

Flowers and plants are elements every home should include. They not only make you feel good mentally, but also can go with any type of interior style.

Most interior design books and interior designers say that faux flowers are a big no-no in a home. They say fake flowers are tacky and one should invest in buying new flowers every week.

If we lived in a perfect world, then sure, I'd agree with that advice. However, we don't live in a perfect world, and not everyone has the time or budget to go out and purchase dozens of flowers every week. I hear this constantly: "You can even go to your local grocery store and get flowers for ten dollars." Let me break down the math: Most people have more than one vase in their home. If you have three, as an example, that's about thirty dollars per week you're spending on flowers, which is about $1,560 per year. That's a lot of money!

Faux flowers are the way to go to save time and money. Head to your local craft store and find some pretty faux camellias, hydrangeas, or peonies. If your vases are clear, buy an acrylic water kit or fill your vases up with new water each week. If you have the time and money to purchase real flowers each week, then definitely go for it. But if you can't, and you still want to incorporate flowers into your decor, carefully selected faux flowers can work for you!

Pooling your curtains on the floor can instantly create a luxurious feel in your space.

Neutral colors are the way to go when picking out colors for a sofa. A neutral-colored couch will not only bring out the details in your decor, such as your throw pillows, but also allow you to easily change out your decor throughout the year if you get bored of a particular interior style.

Be sure to choose down-filled throw pillows over cotton ones, as they are more comfortable and can make the sofa look chic. Also make sure not to overdo it with your pillows. If you have a two-seater, four or fewer pillows should be plenty.

If you want to add an extra homey feel to your space, layer a throw blanket over the arm of your sofa. Make sure your throw blanket and pillows are not the same color as your sofa because you don't want those details blending in with each other.

The key to incorporating more seating

into your living room is to include seating which also acts as decor. It's that simple. Chic stools, ottomans, and poufs are great examples of statement pieces that also serve as extra seating.

Many landlords will let
you paint your walls . . .
but have you ever thought
of painting your ceiling?
This can make your space
not only feel larger, but
also more unique.

Need a room divider in a studio? Wardrobe doors are a perfect example of a chic way to divide a living and sleeping space.

You only have so much room to define the space in your home, especially if it's a smaller space. The most important element of decorating is covering your walls with art. Art is not only a reflection of you, but also a reflection of your home. Even just one piece of art can dramatically change the aura of a space instantaneously.

The first mistake anyone can make, whether you live in a large home or small apartment, is leaving a wall bare. Without wall art or decoration, the entire space will feel unfinished. There should always be some type of design element on each wall in your home.

When decorating your walls, don't restrict yourself to just hanging artwork. Mirrors, clocks, wall candles, tapestry, removable wallpaper—all are great examples of other ways you can fill up wall space. You can even hang real wallpaper or fabric using liquid starch! If you want to keep/hang any posters on your walls, make sure they are framed.

I tend to like mirrors as alternatives to art because they create the illusion of a larger space. You can also hang shelves where you can place decor or artwork for a chic effect.

Lastly, wall art/decor is something you should splurge on if you want to. Because it's not constantly touched, it can be used for years and taken from home to home. If you don't have a definite style or don't want to spend too much on art, you can still find wonderfully priced pieces online or at your local discount store.

ALTERNATIVES TO NAILING INTO WALLS

Although many landlords will allow tenants to nail into walls, there are some that don't permit it. Here are a few ways you can display your art while leaving your walls damage-free.

If you are set on hanging your art, removable adhesive hooks and Velcro strips are a great alternative to nails.

If you have art that is too heavy to be held by anything adhesive, below are a few ways you can still display your accents:

- Leaned on top of a surface such as a console
- Displayed on an étagère or bookshelf
- Placed on an art easel
- Leaned against the wall on the floor

PINK HOTEL

NASHVILLE

Wainscoting or panel molding is the perfect addition to make a space feel more luxurious and historic. This character feature has always been known as a project that can only be completed in an owned space, but today, I'm going to break that myth. Here is an easy way you can apply wainscoting in your rental without causing any damage to your walls.

To add wainscoting to your space, you'll need two items:

- Removable corner Velcro tape
- Wall panels made from a light material

First, you'll need to purchase wall panels (or a wall panel kit) that are made from a light material such as urethane. Traditional plaster or wood will be too heavy for this project. It's also important to make sure that the panels are completely flat on the back and have no indent.

You'll also need to buy removable Velcro tape that can hold up to four pounds per strip. I recommend getting corner Velcro tape!

Apply the Velcro tape to each corner of the wall panel. Next, secure the panel on the wall by putting pressure on it for thirty seconds.

Dreamed of having a chandelier? You can use a plug-in pendant and swag it on the ceiling. Just make sure to clear it with your landlord first since you will need to drill a hole in the ceiling for the hook.

The first thing people ask me when walking into my home is, "How in the world are you allowed to put up wallpaper in a rented apartment?" They are always shocked when I tell them it's not wallpaper—it's tape!

To create the same type of look I crafted in my living room, you'll need two items:

- Tape
- Scissors

I went with a gold metallic tape, but you can pretty much use any kind, as long as it's not permanent and does not leave residue. The tape I chose was a half inch wide, but you can definitely use tape as wide as one inch if you want a more dramatic look or have a wider wall.

The trick to creating straight lines with no wrinkles or creases is to secure the tape on one edge of the wall and slowly unroll the tape until you reach the other side of the wall. Then, you use your scissors and cut the tape. It's crucial to unroll the tape slowly.

Plants are a great way to add a pop of color in a mostly neutral space.

Everyone wants to have a space that's warm, comfortable, and cozy. Having that "homey" feel not only makes you feel good, but it also makes your space more inviting for your guests.

Luxe fabrics.

Faux fur, velvet, and suede are fabrics that will instantly give your space a cozy lift. Add some faux fur pillows to your couch or incorporate a suede ottoman in the space.

Down pillows.

Nothing says cozy more than a bunch of fluffy pillows! I prefer down inserts over cotton or polyester because they mold and can be shaped. You always want to be able to "fluff" your pillows.

Throw blankets.

Blankets are key to creating an inviting space. Layer a throw over the arm of your couch or keep a blanket peeking out of a wicker basket.

Warm lighting.

When choosing lighting for your space, aim for soft white bulbs. Warm lighting promotes calmness and relaxation.

Touch of leather.

Leather, no matter what the color is, will instantly warm up your space. You can invest in a leather pouf or layer a leather pillow over your couch.

Don't have enough cabinet space? A bar cart isn't only a chic decorative statement, but it also doubles as a place to store glassware.

Nowadays, it's very common to work from home. Whether working from home is a once-a-week or daily occurrence, it's so important to have a comfortable space to work from. Unfortunately, if you're living in a small house or apartment, you may not have the luxury of a dedicated work area. The tips below will help ensure those who live in small spaces can still easily work from home.

Make sure you have a hard surface to work on.

Whether it's a stand-up tray or a foldable table, make sure you have some type of a flat surface to work on. Coffee tables are just a bit too low to work at comfortably. Aim for something high enough so you're not bending down to read or to look at a computer.

De-clutter your space.

Miscellaneous items lying around the area you're working in can be a huge distraction. Make sure to tidy up before starting your work to avoid any distractions or triggers for stress.

Embrace natural light.

If possible, try to work in an area with natural light. This will give you a boost of happiness and will make your work more productive, as well.

Make your bed.

Do you have to work from bed with a stand-up tray? Make your bed before you start to work. This will help prevent you from wanting to snuggle up and fall asleep. Also make sure you have a supportive pillow behind you while working.

Hang a large to-do list.

Keep a large to-do list hanging in the space where you're working. This allows you to see the tasks you need to complete easily and will help you from feeling overwhelmed. In addition, a to-do list will help inspire you to finish your work ASAP.

Move the remotes.

Working in a space with a TV? Move the remote to the other side of the home so there's no temptation!

Buy noise-canceling headphones.

If there's noise in the home you can't get away from, make sure to invest in noise-canceling headphones.

Work in a space with neutral colors.

If your bedroom is full of bright pops of color, you might want to stay away from that area when working. It's scientifically proven that you will work more productively in an area with neutral, calming colors.

If you must work from your bed, a stand-up tray is essential.

Need extra storage space? Bar cabinets and buffet tables can be utilized for items such as clothing, electronics, dishware, etc.

Feeling moody but live in a small space? A large mirror is the perfect contrast to a darker wall color and will make the room feel more spacious.

Layering rugs is a fabulous way to add a chic, unique statement to your space.

KITCHEN

BEFORE

Having a rented kitchen can be frustrating: You can't knock down walls or replace ugly countertops. Most people just give up on even trying to decorate their kitchen due to these restrictions. However, even with these limitations, you can still achieve a beautiful kitchen with a little bit of creativity and patience.

Cover your countertops with contact paper.

Contact paper is an excellent alternative for covering up your not-so-modern countertop. There are endless patterns that mimic popular textures. Clean and dry before starting the application, and be sure to research the correct application process before starting. Once you are ready to remove your contact paper upon moving out, make sure to have adhesive remover on hand for some cleanup!

Replace the hardware.

Consider replacing knobs and handles on the kitchen drawers. Even if changing the hardware is all you do in the space, it can still create a dramatic transformation. Just remember to keep the originals for when you eventually move out.

Invest in removable backsplash tile.

Nowadays, there are many budget-friendly options for removable accents that look just like the real thing! From a subway pattern to mosaic tile, you can have the backsplash you've always dreamed of having without driving your landlord crazy.

Cover your floors.

Ugly floor tiles are an eyesore. A rug is a perfect option to hide any unsightly floors. If you're feeling ambitious, you can also invest in some removable floor tiles or a vinyl floor cloth.

Add shelf risers.

Shelf risers are useful for making better use of limited space and keeping your kitchen organized. You can use them in your pantry, cabinets, and even refrigerator.

Incorporate art.

Make sure to incorporate some elements of art and decor in the space. You can display framed artwork on a wall in your kitchen or a small accent piece on your countertop.

Display chic organizers.

Don't have room in your drawers for your spatulas? Buy a cute utensil holder to display on your countertop. It's important to keep everything on your kitchen surface as pleasing to the eye as possible.

Remove the cabinet doors.

Open shelving, even though harder to maintain, will give the illusion that your space is larger than it actually is.

BEFORE

Lacking counterspace?

You can buy a board to place over your sink or make one yourself! I cut a wooden board a little wider than the size of my sink and styled it the same as my countertop by using contact paper.

Open shelving will make your space feel more glamorous and give the illusion that the area is larger than it actually is.

BEFORE

If you live in a smaller home, you might not have the luxury of having space for a proper dining table. The alternatives below will ensure you always have a hard surface to eat on.

Wall-mounted folding table.

This is a fabulous way to still have a proper table to eat at without wasting any space. This item allows you to fold up your table into a wall when you're not eating to save loads of usable space.

Folding tray table.

I am definitely not talking about the gaudy tray tables we always see on TV. You can get a chic, foldable tray table to store until you need it.

Small rolling island.

A small, rolling island can not only be a surface to prepare food on, but also a usable space where you can eat your meals. Some islands actually have stools built into them!

Lift-top coffee table.

This type of coffee table allows you to eat your food at a normal height and gives you plenty of storage within the piece.

Stand-up tray.

If you love eating on your couch and your coffee table is too low for your liking, try a stand-up tray. It will allow you to eat your food at a comfortable height and is super easy to store.

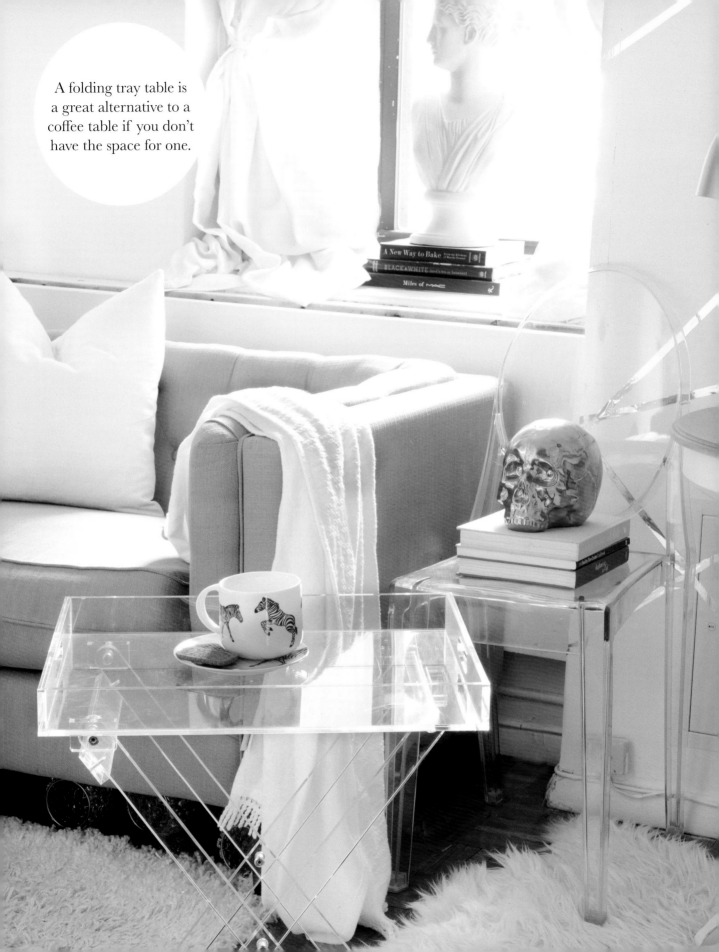

A folding tray table is a great alternative to a coffee table if you don't have the space for one.

BEDROOM /

It *is* possible to convince your landlord to let you do actual renovations. Some landlords will allow you to add real wainscoting, switch out countertops, or even completely renovate a bathroom.

Whether you negotiate for them to pay for it or you have to chip in, these are considered upgrades that will keep their property competitive. All you have to do is ask your landlord if it's okay. The worst they can say is no!

I believe your bedroom is the most special room of your home. You spend approximately one-third of your life asleep, which means you spend one-third of your life in the bedroom. That's a huge chunk of time! The bedroom should be designed as your sanctuary; it is a place where you go to de-stress, not create it. This is usually the only space in your home you can make your own, especially if you're living with a roommate.

When designing your bedroom, it's better to remain more neutral. Your bedroom should always have a calming, relaxed aura to it. I like to suggest sticking to grays, whites, and blues when decorating a bedroom.

For bedding, I always say white on white is key. Years ago, I would have shuddered at that thought! First, white will always go with everything. If you ever get tired of a particular style in your bedroom, all you have to do is switch out the smaller items such as throw pillows and decor. Second, white is very easy to clean because you can wash it at high temperatures. Third, it can make a smaller room feel larger as white will always create the illusion of a bigger space. Finally, it will make your bedroom feel luxe as white bedding is very hotel-like.

As for decor and art, it's also best to stay neutral and chic. You do not want to overdo it with decor and art because you don't want your bedroom feeling cluttered. Clutter will create a stressful environment, and you definitely want tranquility in this space!

Neutral-colored bedding will make your bedroom feel grander.

Not allowed to paint? Removable wallpaper is a great alternative for covering up that wall color you just can't stand!

Don't have enough room for a proper dresser? A narrow floating shelf and mirror can give you the space you need to get ready.

Dedicated spot for hair products.

Keeping your room clean and organized is key to creating a stress-free space. Instead of having all of your hair products and appliances scattered on top of a dresser, keep a box, bin, or basket nearby to house those products.

Vase of flowers.

Nothing says happiness more than flowers. They will not only put a smile on your face, but also add a chic feel to any space.

Throw pillows.

No bed is complete without a good set of throw pillows. There isn't a set rule as to how many or how few throw pillows you have, as long as they balance your space and are easy to care for. I recommend throw pillows with a removable cover so you can wash as needed.

Air purifier.

Who wants to breathe in dust and dead skin cells at night? Keeping a small air purifier in your bedroom will ensure that the air is clean and will help prevent dust buildup on your furniture.

Tray.

This is truly a multi-functional item. You can use a tray for decor, eating, working, and so on.

Miscellaneous bin.

A miscellaneous box or basket will help prevent clutter around your bedroom.

Whenever you feel lazy and don't feel like putting an item back, throw it in the basket. Just be certain to put everything back where it belongs once the basket becomes full.

Small tray for jewelry.

Make sure you have a dedicated spot for all the small pieces of jewelry you wear day to day. This will help you keep track of where your items are and help keep your dresser less cluttered.

If your room is smaller and the bed needs

to be placed in a corner, install a small shelf on the wall adjacent to the bed. You can place small items of decor on it until you have a specific need for the space.

WHY YOU SHOULD USE A DUVET COVER

I know what you're thinking: duvets are a pain. However, if you live in an apartment, I recommend buying a duvet cover and using a comforter inside of it.

It's so much easier to wash and dry a duvet cover than a comforter. If you're living in an apartment building, you probably have an in-building laundry room, or you go to a laundromat every week. The washers and dryers in buildings are most likely going to be small, and there's a very good chance your comforter will not fit. Dragging a full-sized comforter to a laundromat is not an easy chore. When you use a duvet cover, you'll only have to wash the cover; the comforter inside will remain clean.

To be precise, there is a difference between a duvet insert and a duvet cover. A duvet cover is an enclosed cover in which you can stuff your comforter inside and seal it. It is often constructed of the same types of fabrics as sheets. The duvet insert is typically a blanket or comforter. You don't even have to buy a duvet insert. You can use the comforter you currently have and just buy a duvet cover to encase it.

Mirrors are a great way to make a smaller room look larger. Fun tip: A taller mirror will make your ceiling height seem grander.

The first step to decorating your dresser

is to find a chic mirror to lean on or hang above it. Make sure you find a mirror that's proportional to your dresser. Next, it's important to add one or two small accents to the top of your dresser such as a candle or small piece of decor. You want this piece of furniture to be functional and stylish.

Additionally, you can also switch out the hardware (i.e., drawer pulls or knobs) to add more dimension to the piece.

IDEAS FOR ROOM DIVIDERS

As you can see here, a room divider, made from wardrobe doors, was used to create a bedroom in a studio apartment. Below are some ideas on how to create a faux wall like this one.

- Wardrobe doors
- Curtains
- Bookshelves
- Folding screens

I know this topic was broadly discussed much earlier in the book, but now I want to go into greater detail about the bedroom.

Mattress.

Invest. You sleep one-third of your life. You want to make sure that you find a mattress that not only is comfortable, but will last through the years.

Sheets.

Invest. Quality bed linens can mean the difference between a restful night and a night spent tossing and turning. This also applies to duvet covers.

Throw Blanket.

Do not invest. A throw blanket will primarily be used for decoration or perhaps an extra layer at night when cold. This is definitely an item you don't need to spend hundreds on.

Throw Pillows.

Do not invest. Throw pillows are used often and will eventually become dirty over time. Buy new, inexpensive throw pillows/pillow covers at discount stores or on Amazon.

Comforter Insert.

Invest. I know inserts are crazy expensive, but the fill of them is so important. I recommend getting a pure down comforter. Nothing will beat the comfort and it will be nice and cozy during the winter!

Headboard.

Either/or. If you do fall in love with a bed frame or headboard, you can definitely invest as long as you know you won't be changing bed sizes anytime soon.

Dresser.

Do not invest. Your dresser is an item that will be used continuously, especially if that's the area where you get ready in the morning. Make sure not to spend too much money on this item, because you're probably going to need to switch it out after a few years.

Nightstand.

Either/or. I frequently use my nightstand when I eat meals from my bed. I'm always spilling liquids and foods on it, which is the reason I personally don't like investing in this item. If you only use your nightstand for a cup of water or electronics, then feel free to spend more on one.

If someone asked me my favorite staple decor, it would definitely be books. No home is complete without a good set of "coffee-table books" to display. Many people have the opinion that books are meant for just coffee tables and bookshelves; however, they can also be displayed many different ways.

Under decor.

This is one of my favorite design tips. Take a stack of two to three books and place them under a piece of decor. This works great on furniture like console tables and bar carts.

Under a lamp.

Give your lamp some extra height and glam by layering a few books underneath.

On the floor.

Stack some books on the floor and add a plant or small statue on top. You can use this method in a non-working fireplace to give your space an extra-cozy feel.

In a fireplace.

No, I don't mean you should burn your books! Many older apartments have fireplaces that no longer function. Placing a stack of books in a non-working fireplace will give your space an extra touch of charm and character.

BATHROOM

Removable floor tile
or vinyl can instantly
transform the look of
your bathroom. Your
guests will be in awe!

BEFORE

Like rented kitchens, rental bathrooms can be difficult to style and enhance. It's definitely discouraging when you look at dream bathrooms on Pinterest and realize that you can't tear everything out and begin again. Nonetheless, even though you can't formally renovate the space, you can still make changes that will result in a stunning impact.

Switch out the shower curtain to reflect your own unique style. This is a simple, quick, and cost-effective improvement when you can't paint your walls or remove ugly tile. A shower curtain can instantly change the look of your space.

Try covering up those unsightly floor tiles with a rug, removable floor tile or a vinyl floor covering. Ugly wall tile or color? Use framed art to disguise the imperfections of your walls or add shelves with decor on them. You can even apply removable wallpaper!

Unappealing countertops can easily be covered with contact paper. I suggest white marble contact paper if it's a smaller space, as it will make the space feel grander and larger.

If you're in need of more storage, as most of us are, make sure to opt for visually pleasing pieces like woven baskets and cute shelving. This not only keeps a bathroom clutter-free, but also adds a chic feel to the space.

Adding small (or large if there's space!) accents is a great way to incorporate more character and dimension to this room. Candles, plants, and small items of decor are great examples of accents that will accomplish this purpose.

If you want, you can even switch out the light fixtures in your bathroom as long as you switch them back to the original upon moving out. Just make sure to get approval from your landlord first!

Finally, it's important to remember to stick to a color palette that complements what's already there. If you fight what's already there, it might make the space feel more chaotic than it actually is.

A bold paint color can make an extra-bland bathroom feel extra-luxurious. You can even ask your landlord for permission to switch out the existing mirror.

White towels.

Nothing will make your bathroom feel more spa-like than fresh, white towels. Keep towels on display and easily accessible for guests. Also make sure to roll instead of fold for design and storage. Additionally, always keep nice, soft hand towels out for you and your guests. Not having hand towels out means that your guests will wipe their hands on your bath towels and you definitely don't want that!

Bottle of nice lotion.

It's always nice to keep a full bottle of lotion in your bathroom for guests after they wash their hands or have showered. Your guests will really appreciate it!

Decorative books.

Not only are books great for decoration, they can also be extremely functional! It's always nice to have something to read or browse through when taking a long bath or visiting the porcelain throne.

Flowers.

Every room can benefit from flowers or a plant. Not only are they relaxing, but they are beautiful to look at, as well.

STORAGE

If you live in a smaller space, you've probably had an issue with storage at some point. This may not come as a surprise to you, but the key to having enough storage is knowing how to *organize*.

You should absolutely take advantage of organizers such as shelf risers, drawer dividers, drawer organizers, and lazy Susans in your home. These items are a lifesaver when it comes to saving space in cabinets, closets, and drawers. I personally swear by shelf risers. I use them in *literally* every closet and cabinet in my home. Other great space-saver items are removable hooks. These are so versatile, can be used anywhere in the home, don't require nails, and can be easily removed when your lease is up. You can use them to hang rags in your kitchen or on the side of your dresser to hold your heat appliances (hair dryer, curler). The possibilities are endless!

Items such as cute jars and wicker baskets are not only great for storage but also work as fabulous design elements, as well. Adding a wicker basket in your bathroom will add a spa-like feel to the space while giving you a dedicated spot for your toilet paper or towels.

Another key to acquiring more storage in your home is to use the decor and furniture you already have as storage. You can use the space under your bed or couch and above cabinets to store items. You can even utilize the space behind furniture. Make sure to keep everything stored under, over, or behind furniture in plastic containers, bins, or wrapping to prevent dust buildup over time. Nowadays, you can even find an endless amount of furniture with built-in storage such as ottomans, beds, or even couches.

If you really don't have space for something, display it proudly! For example, if you don't have enough space in your closet for your clothes and shoes, display some outside your closet as a chic feature. Do you have a lot of books and not know where to store them all? Use them as decoration. Place some under a lamp or display them on a console table.

Shelf risers are a necessity in any closet or cabinet. They maximize space by creating easy access to items and allowing you to double the amount you can store.

Don't have a closet? Wardrobes or clothing racks are fabulous alternatives to store your clothes.

DE-CLUTTERING YOUR LIVING ROOM

I know how difficult it is to keep everything organized, especially if you're living in a smaller space. You clean one day, and a day later everything is in complete chaos. Through living and learning, I've found the perfect balance between style and functionality in the living room.

Raise your hand if you've ever lost the remote. I might not be able to see you, but I know there are some hands up in the air right now. Most of us leave our remotes somewhere on the couch or coffee table. After years of losing my remotes between seat cushions and under tables, I needed an alternative solution. The key is to have a dedicated spot for them: find a cute, small jar, bin, or container that is solely dedicated for remote controls. Keep this container either on your coffee table or somewhere near your TV. After a few days or weeks, you're going to subconsciously put the remotes back into that dedicated spot.

Another problem many people encounter in their living room is clothing clutter. What I mean by this is all of the shoes, jackets, socks, and other assorted clothing items that slowly appear over time in this particular area of the home. The trick is to keep a small/medium-sized "miscellaneous bin" in the living room. This is now where all of those items will go—and as soon as it's filled to the top, you know it's time to clean it out. I also use this method in my bedroom. It's great for those lazy days when you just don't want to put any clothes back in the closet!

My next trick for a de-cluttered living room is hiding electrical or charging cords with decor. It's amazing how much cleaner a room can feel without a bunch of black, ugly cords in sight. Find a cute piece of decor or an object to block these wires or you can go the traditional route and use wire covers. I promise this will make a world of difference!

Besides the floor, your dresser is probably going to be the most cluttered area in the bedroom. It's where we fix our hair, apply our makeup, and put on our clothes every single day. For most of us, it's not just the top of the dresser that gets cluttered, but the interior of the drawers, as well. With these tips, organizing those drawers and de-cluttering the top of your dresser can be a pain-free process.

Remove all items from drawers.

Before you start organizing the contents within the drawers, make sure you remove everything beforehand. It'll be a nightmare if you try to organize while all your items are still inside.

Use drawer dividers.

Drawer dividers allow you to easily add different categories of clothing in a single drawer. For example, I use a drawer divider to split up my tank tops and T-shirts.

Invest in a makeup organizer.

Makeup organizers will give you a dedicated space for all your makeup, helping you avoid clutter on the surface.

Roll-not-fold.

The number-one hack to saving space in a drawer is to roll your clothes instead of folding them.

Keep most-used items on top.

Do you rarely wear jeans but always wear leggings? Keep your leggings in one of the top drawers and jeans at the bottom. This allows easy access to items you normally use day to day.

These tips are not just useful for your dresser, but also any used drawers within your home.

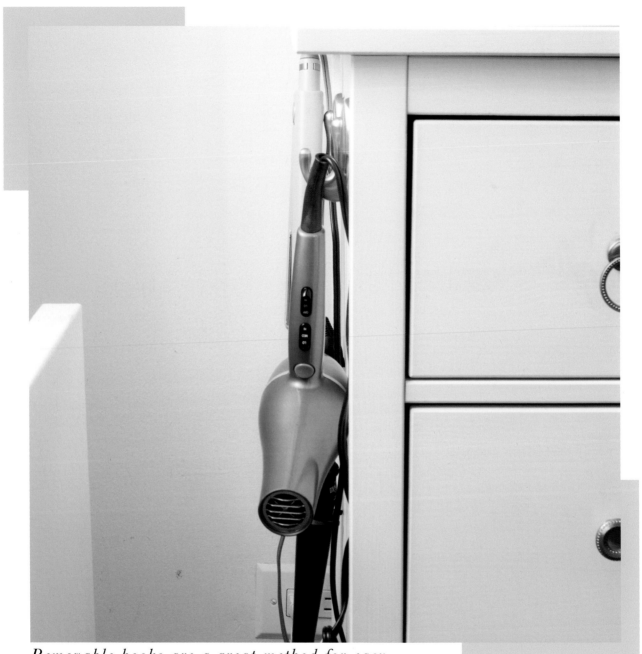

Removable hooks are a great method for easy access to everyday items.

Storage-turned-furniture is key for smaller spaces.

Use door space for extra storage.

Whether it's installing small bins or using an over-the-door shoe rack, the vertical space on your doors is a great area for extra storage. Another go-to trick is hanging Command hooks on the inside of cabinet doors to store rags, notes, scarves—whatever.

Invest in a file cabinet.

If I had to choose only one organizational accessory for the home, it would have to be a file cabinet or file box. We all have bills, instructions, receipts, coupons, tax records, and other paperwork that ends up being piled together in a random drawer or bin. By the time you end up needing a certain document, you can never find it! A file cabinet or file system will drastically make your life feel more organized and less chaotic.

Store behind curtains.

Behind curtains is a great area to store decor, artwork, bags, and other small or thin items. A little secret of mine is that I store an item behind every curtain in my home.

Find unexpected places for storage.

Have space between your refrigerator and wall? What about space above your kitchen cabinets? These are fabulous places to store items. You can even use a crevice between two pieces of furniture to store thinner items such as trays and bags.

HOSTING

We all love that feeling of being the host and having friends and family over. I personally adore planning parties and weekend brunches at my place. Some of you might find it a scary thought to host a gathering in a space you feel is too small. Well, now it's time to dispose of that fear, because there's no such thing as having too small of a space to host.

Always prepare food and drinks.

The first thing to remember is to set out food and drinks before people arrive no matter how small or large the gathering is. Even if it's just one friend stopping by, he/she will always remember you as the host who went out of their way. Go-to food and drinks for hosting are sparkling water, wine, cheese, crackers, and veggies.

Utilize surface area.

It's important to use every surface in your home when hosting a larger party. Store away your appliances and large pieces of decor and replace them with decorative dishes, glasses, and platters. Tiered cake stands and tray risers are other great options to save space. In addition, it's nice to keep a chic tray table stored away when you absolutely need more surface space. Having an intimate dinner party but lack a dining table? No problem! You can use your coffee table as a place for your guests to eat.

Have a dedicated spot for coats.

When having a larger gathering, it's important to have a dedicated spot to place coats and bags instead of having those items scattered across the home. A bench near the doorway or a bedroom are great areas for these items.

Incorporate some design.

Even if only one person is coming over, it's always important to put in that extra effort. Whether it's by adding garnishes to cocktails, incorporating chic centerpieces, or serving on decorative plates, the extra effort won't be forgotten by your guest(s).

Provide glass name tags.

A functional and stylish touch to any large gathering is to provide name tags and pens for people to mark their cocktail glasses. Drinks can easily get mixed up in a smaller space, and this method is a great way to prevent that from happening.

Control flow of traffic.

Another rule for hosting in a smaller space is to control the flow of traffic. This means keeping your food, say, in the kitchen, and drinks in the living room, so one place isn't too congested. A bar cart or console table is a great place to lay out drink options.

Let some air in.

It's important to let some air in, especially when you're hosting a larger party. Open your windows or invest in some fans you can spread throughout your home so guests don't get too hot.

Keep a folding table stored away.

Typically, in a smaller space, there's not too much surface area to use for a party. If you're hosting a large gathering, invest in a folding table you can take out for these large events.

A folding table is a necessity in every small space. Keep it stored away until you need it—for studying, a party, etc.

GO-TO RESOURCES

Amazon
Amazon is probably the first place I head to if I want something very specific. I love Prime two-day shipping.

HomeGoods
This is one of my favorite stores in the entire world. The best days to shop here are during mornings on weekdays.

T.J. Maxx
Less stock than HomeGoods but the same quality of items. Some of my favorite decor pieces are from T.J. Maxx.

Cost Plus World Market
This is a great place to get high-quality furniture on a low-end budget.

H&M Home
This is my go-to store for small items of decor and chic kitchen accessories.

Etsy
Etsy is the best resource for unique wallpaper and decor.

CB2
Modern-meets-budget at CB2. The deals here are amazing.

Z Gallerie
For all things glam, Z Gallerie is your place.

Target
I could browse Target's deals for hours. Also make sure you check out their inventory online as well as in the store.

Wayfair
I always recommend Wayfair for large items of furniture. They have fabulous shipping times.

Home Depot
This is one of my go-to places for hardware, lighting, and paint.

West Elm
West Elm always has fabulous sales and their inventory is made from high-end materials.

TOV
TOV is one of my favorite brands to turn to if I am looking for something unique and budget-friendly.

ACKNOWLEDGMENTS

I have to give a few people shout-outs, because if it weren't for some, this book would have never happened. First, I would like to thank Sara, Jackie, and Kat for letting me into your home and helping you create beauty out of it. Thank you, Carly and Kathy, for giving me the opportunity to photograph your charming homes.

I would also like to thank Alisa, Autumn, Shweta, Baylee, Carrie, Christina, Ellenor, Hannah Skaar, Ola, Jessica, Jolie, Hoda, Kathleen, Kristina, Linnea, Madison, Miranda, Natalia, Nicole, Paige, Samantha, Sandra, Sarah, Lauren, Stefanie, and Corinne for contributing your beautiful spaces and projects to this book. Your homes and designs are a wonderful representation of clever, small-space interiors. Pauline, Rachel, and Sara, thank you for the countless amount of support you've offered me over the past year. I am beyond lucky to have you in my life.

I would like to thank my wonderful parents for always believing in me and teaching me that there is no secret to success; it's purely a result of hard work and learning from failure. Being a "helicopter parent" ended up working out to my benefit. Your continued support, dedication, and advice is what encourages me to succeed beyond my goals. And a big thank-you to Annie, my agent, for always believing in me and this project. Words can't express how much gratitude I have for you. Additionally, a big thank you to my editor, Nicole Frail, for all the support you've shown me through this journey.

Most importantly, I have to thank my readers of *City Chic Decor*. The most beautiful and magical part of working on the blog is receiving messages, comments, and emails from you, stating that I helped or inspired you in some way.

I am truly beyond grateful for all of you and hope this book makes you proud.

PHOTO CREDITS

ABOUT THE AUTHOR

CHELSEY BROWN is an interior decorator living in Manhattan. Chelsey started her blog, *City Chic Decor* (citychicdecor.com), when she realized how little information there was on decorating and designing rented spaces. Soon after starting the blog, she was designing and decorating apartments all over New York City and the United States. Chelsey's designs, writing, and photography have been featured in countless publications, print magazines, and online resources such as the *Today Show, Small Space Makeovers* magazine, *Flea Market Style* magazine, *Apartment Therapy, The Everygirl, The Kitchn,* and *Inspired by This.* Additionally, Chelsey has been nominated for four awards and won Interior Decorating Blog of the Year and Excellence in Affordable E-Design Services by *Build* magazine. She has also collaborated with big-name brands such as, Pier 1 Imports, HomeGoods, Sleep Number, StreetEasy, Wayfair, Mr. Coffee, and Poshmark.

INDEX